WHERE'S DADDY?

By

Shauna Lee Daddabbo

Illustrations by Amina Yaqoob

WHERE'S DADDY?

Copyright © 2021 by Shauna Lee Daddabbo
Illustrations by Amina Yaqoob

All rights reserved. This book or any portion thereof
may not be reproduced or used in any manner whatsoever
without the express written permission of the publisher
except for the use of brief quotations in a book review.

ISBN: 978-0-578-98689-0

To My Children,
Savauni, Saviyaun and Kaivaun
You're my rock,
my tick to my clock
My heart & soul,
the reason I met this goal.
I love you!
MOM

To My Dad,
Thanks for all that you do
and displaying courage.
You taught me so much
including to always
help others.

Love You!

This Book belongs to

____

Saviy was home, and playing one day.
She loved building with blocks, and sculpting with clay.

She loved to play soccer, she danced and she drew.
She loved singing and science, and outer space too.

But when she played house, with her dolls in a row.
There was always one question, she wanted to know.

She had a doll for herself, and her mom was there too.
But the one thing she wondered, but still never knew.
Was, "Where was her daddy?", Why wasn't he there?
Does he know that she misses him? Does he know that she cares?

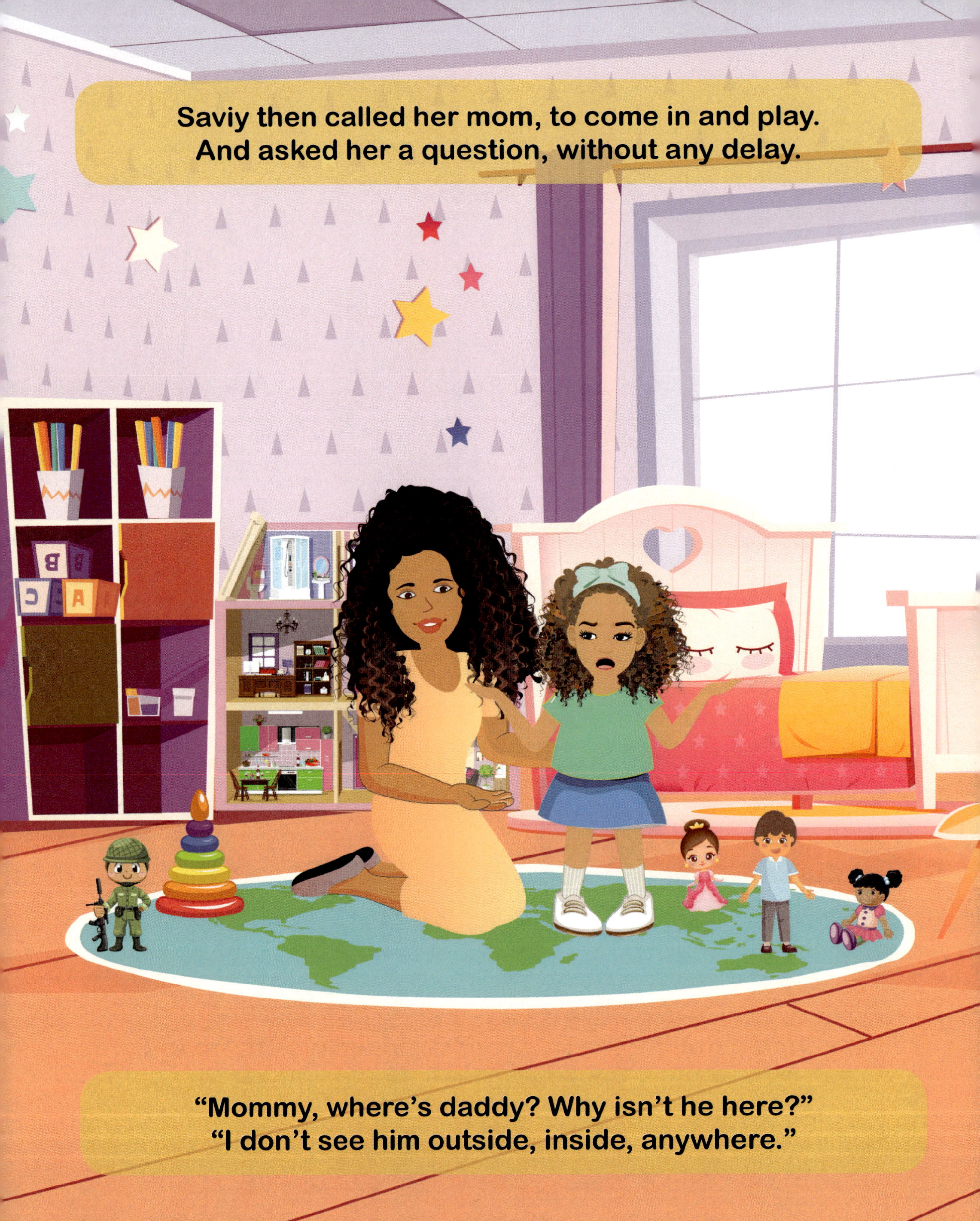
Saviy then called her mom, to come in and play.
And asked her a question, without any delay.
"Mommy, where's daddy? Why isn't he here?"
"I don't see him outside, inside, anywhere."

"Oh Saviy," said mommy sitting down on the ground.
"There are so many reasons, daddies may not be around."
"You know that I love you, with all of my heart."
"And we'll always be together, and never apart."

Saviy's mom told her daughter, even though he's away.
She tries her hardest, each night and each day.
"Don't worry sweet Saviy, we'll both be alright."
Then she gave her a kiss, and hugged her real tight.

"Now here are some reasons why daddies aren't home."
"Maybe they're traveling, to England or Rome."

"Maybe they're flying, a jet in the sky."
"Or driving a truck, full of building supplies."

"Some dads work on boats, or have jobs far away."
"They may leave for a month, or a couple of days."

APRIL
1 2 3 4 5
6 7 8 9 10 11
12 13 14 15 16
18 19 20 21 22 23
24 25 26 27 28

Saviy's mom explained all this could take dads away.
But they still love their kids, and they wish they could stay.

Saviy was starting, to understand why.
She looked at her mom, and began to reply.
"Like some dads in the military, they travel so far."
"To a place you can't get, in a bus or a car."

"Or dads that play sports, might be out on the road."
She understood now, and it started to show.

Maybe some dads, have to travel around.
Singing or acting, in all different towns.

Some dads and moms, may just not live together.
Sometimes this arrangement, just works out much better.

Sometimes a dad, may look down from above.
Watching over you daily, with guidance and love.

If you haven't met yet, then maybe someday.
Tomorrow is hopeful, in most every way.
"But no matter the cause, or where they may be."
"Your dad always loves you, my little Saviy."

Saviy looked happy, with the talk they just had.
It answered her question, regarding her dad.

She hugged her mom tightly, to show that she cared.
She knew that she loved her, and would always be there.

"Mommy," said Saviy, "For all that you do,"
"I want to say one thing, and that's I love you."

"Thank you for doing, for giving and caring."
"Thank you for loving me, teaching me, sharing."

Saviy knew then, that it was alright.
Her mom was her rock, and tomorrow was bright.
love
Saviy kept playing, this time with a smile.
If she saw her dad soon, or not for a while.
She knew things would work out, they'd both be OK.
With her mom by her side, taking it day by day.

ABOUT THE AUTHOR

Shauna Daddabbo born and raised in Boston, Massachusetts, is the author of children's book ***"Where's Daddy?"*** She dedicates her work to the children of her youth mentoring program, Divas Mentoring Divas Inc. Through engaging short stories and delightful poetry, Shauna addresses the common questions, sticky situations, and complex topics her young mentees encounter.

From a young age, Shauna has loved writing music and poetry. She now incorporates her writing talent into her performing art programs, workshops, workbooks, and online courses. A mother of two girls, and one boy, Shauna resides with her family in Atlanta, Georgia, where she enjoys writing and mentoring. Ms. Daddabbo stays busy as a life coach, business strategist, and winemaker, among her many other trades and business ventures.

If you want to know more about the energetic Shauna Daddabbo, please visit her website at www.MsDaddabbo.com

Made in the USA
Middletown, DE
25 September 2021